Disastrous
Volcanoes

by Melvin Berger

Franklin Watts
New York/London/Toronto/Sydney/1981
A First Book

Photographs courtesy of
the Federal Emergency Management Agency:
opp. p. 1; Hawaii Visitors Bureau: p. 6; National
Park Service: p. 19 (photo by Garrett Smathens);
U.S. Geological Survey: pp. 24, 25, 56, 59, 62;
n.c.: p. 31; National Archives: p. 35; U.S. Air
Force: p. 38; Universal Studios: p. 46.

Maps and diagram by Vantage Art, Inc.

Cover photograph courtesy of
United Press International

Opposite page 1: the May 18, 1980,
eruption of Mount St. Helens.

Library of Congress Cataloging in Publication Data

Berger, Melvin.
Disastrous volcanoes.

(A first book)
Includes index.
Summary: Discusses the formation, types,
and locations of volcanoes and describes
the eruptions of Parícutin, Vesuvius, Krakatoa,
Mont Pelée, and Mount St. Helens.
1. Volcanoes—Juvenile literature.
[1. Volcanoes] I. Title.

QE521.3.B47	551.2'1	81–2995
ISBN 0–531–04329–0		AACR2

Contents

Disastrous Volcanoes

1

An American Volcano Erupts

"Oh dear God, this is hell! It's very, very hard to breathe and very dark. If I could only breathe air. God, just give me a breath."

David Crockett, TV photographer for KOMO-TV in Seattle, Washington, shouted these words into the microphone of his sound camera at exactly 8:39 A.M., on Sunday morning, May 18, 1980. He was standing at the foot of Mount St. Helens volcano in the state of Washington. A huge explosion had just blown the entire top off the cone-shaped peak. As he watched in terror and disbelief he felt himself being burned and bruised by a shower of hot ash. The mountain was erupting, and he was right in the middle of it!

Crockett had been sent to the scene because Mount St. Helens had been rumbling and giving signs of coming to life after having been quiet for more than a hundred years. On March 27, 1980, a column of steam and dust rose up from its peak. More small eruptions followed. There were reports of trembling and earth tremors around the area. Crockett's assignment had been to get a few shots of the mountain for a later telecast.

Soon after Crockett arrived at the base of Mount St. Helens to photograph the restless mountain, a really powerful jolt shook the ground on which he was standing. Barely minutes later, the mountain quite literally blew its stack. In a powerful blast, estimated to have the force of a 50-megaton hydrogen bomb, the entire top of Mount St. Helens shot up into the air. It spewed out about 1.5 cubic miles (5.8 cu km) of rock and debris.

Dark clouds of burning hot ash rose 12 miles (19 km) into the sky, bringing complete darkness to the bright May morning. The volcanic ash melted the snow on the mountain, forming rushing rivers of boiling volcanic mud that thundered down the slopes and threatened to bury Crockett alive.

Fortunately for the reporter, a slight rise in the ground split the mud flow into two separate streams. Crockett cowered in the space between them, while all around him trees were uprooted and boulders were flung aside in the mad downhill plunge of the steaming, smelly mud. Trapped in the midst of this inferno, Crockett could only say into his microphone, "Honest to God, I believe I am dead!"

For ten hours Crockett was stuck in this hellish spot. Finally, at 5:30 in the afternoon, a helicopter spotted him in the midst of the wasted landscape. It hovered down, picked him up, and took him to safety.

Crockett had witnessed up close one of the most awesome, frightening, and violent cataclysms of nature—an erupting volcano. Even from a distance it is a terrifying sight.

What causes volcanoes? What materials do volcanoes eject, and where do these materials come from? Where are volcanoes located? Why do they erupt when they do? Are all volcanoes the same? Do they offer any benefits?

For most of history, no one knew the answers to these questions. Volcanoes were surrounded by fear and fantasy. In recent years, though, scientists have begun to explore these remarkable natural occurrences and to understand more and more about them.

2

Origin of Volcanoes

A volcano is an opening in the surface of the earth through which lava, solid rock, and gases are flung up from inside the earth. A volcano is also the mountain of rock that forms around the opening in the earth.

Volcanoes have been around since the earth's creation nearly five billion years ago. The earth's crust, the waters of the oceans, rivers, and lakes, and most of the air we breathe were all derived from volcanic eruptions.

Ever since humans have been on this planet, they have been terrorized by the fury and violence of volcanoes. Ancient peoples invented myths to explain the massive black clouds, the rivers of burning lava, and the giant rockfalls associated with volcanoes.

History and Lore

The ancients made up legends and stories to explain volcanoes and to ease their fears, making it possible for them to live with these frightening and mysterious happenings. Some of the most interesting tales, which are still believed by some, concern Pele, the Polynesian goddess of fire. In one story, Pele was looking for a home on the island of Hawaii. Every time she found a volcano in which she could live, her enemy Kamapuaa, the pig god, who is also associated with the sea, poured water on her. Thus she was forced to move from volcano to volcano. Occasionally in her anger she sent out burning streams of lava, which Kamapuaa promptly quenched with water.

To gain victory over Kamapuaa, Pele changed herself into a beautiful young woman. Kamapuaa fell in love with her, and they married. Whenever Pele grew angry, though, she caused a volcano to erupt in a violent, fiery blaze. Kamapuaa dissolved the marriage and left Pele. To escape her rage he turned himself into a fish called a humu-humu-nuku-nuku-a-puaa. This fish had a very thick skin to withstand the boiling lava that Pele poured into the waters in which he swam.

Even today there are people in Hawaii who try to appease the goddess Pele by throwing pigs or fishes into the craters of volcanoes. They can point out Pele's face in the cloud that forms over erupting volcanoes or in the pools of lava that stream out. For further proof that the goddess really exists, they show tear-shaped bits of lava that they call Pele's tears, and thin lava strands, which are known as Pele's hair.

From another ancient source comes the myth that led to the origin of the word *volcano*. Perhaps 2,500 years ago, the Romans living around the Mediterranean Sea heard rumbling noises and explosive sounds coming from inside the earth. They explained the roar as the clamor made by Vulcan, the god of fire, at work forging thunderbolts for Jupiter, spears and shields for Mars, and arrows for Apollo. When Vulcan stoked the fire in his blacksmith workshop too vigorously, the flames shot up

—5

*According to legend, Pele sent out burning streams
of lava from the volcanoes in which she lived.
In this nighttime photograph, burning lava is
coming from the Kilauea volcano in Hawaii.*

and a volcano erupted. Some say that Vulcan lived in Mount Etna in Sicily. Others believe that his home was Vulcano, one the Lipari Islands near Sicily, which was named after him.

How Volcanoes Are Created

The earth, we know, is a giant ball in space. It is about 8,000 miles (12,800 km) in diameter. The thin outside layer of this ball is the earth's crust. The crust is made up of solid rock, which varies from about 5 to 40 miles (8 to 64 km) in thickness.

Beneath the crust is the mantle, which makes up more than 80 percent of the total volume of the earth. The mantle is about 1,800 miles (2,900 km) thick. It consists of heavy rock that scientists believe is under such terrific heat and pressure that, although it is solid, it is able to change shape.

Even deeper, under the mantle, are the outer core, 1,350 miles (2,160 km) thick, and the inner core, 800 miles (1,280 km) thick. The inner core reaches to the very center of the earth.

Until the 1970s most scientists believed that the earth's crust was a single continuous skin over the entire surface. Scientific findings of the last few years, though, have advanced the theory known as *plate tectonics*. According to plate tectonics theory, the outer layer of the earth is made up of about twelve huge plates of rock. These immense, irregularly shaped blocks float on the heavier rock of the earth's mantle. On their backs, these raftlike plates carry the continents and the oceans that make up the surface of the earth.

Although the plates basically fit into each other like pieces of a giant jigsaw puzzle, each of them is always moving. They move tiny distances—no more than an inch or two (2.5 or 5 cm) a year—so that no one can see or feel them moving. But changes in the face of the earth prove that they do move. Mountains form when two plates collide head on. Ocean valleys are caused when one plate slides under another. Earthquakes occur when plates rub roughly past one another.

Where two plates rub, bump, or push against one another, the leading edge of one plate may be forced down under the edge of the other plate. As the rocks of the first plate descend below the surface, they are subjected to intense heat, which is believed to be due to the radioactivity of the surrounding rocks and to the heat coming from the center of the earth.

In most places, the tremendous pressure beneath the earth's surface prevents the rock from melting despite the great heat, estimated to be at $3,600°$ F ($2,000°$ C). But in a few spots along where the bottom of the crust and the top of the mantle meet, the temperature is high enough and the pressure low enough to melt the solid rock. The melted rock forms pools of nearly liquid molten rock called *magma,* from the Greek word for dough.

Since the magma is lighter than the surrounding solid rock, it tends to rise up toward the surface. It forces its way into any cracks in the rock above. If there are none, it seeks out weak spots where it can split the rock and create its own path. Most of the magma reaches the surface along the edges of the plates, where the crust is weakest and where there are the most fractures in the rock.

The dissolved gases bubble out of the magma with great force, driving it up through a pipelike shaft called a *conduit.* When the magma reaches the surface it is called *lava.* A huge, thick mass of lava explodes out through the opening, known as the *vent.* It rains down over the surrounding area, leaving a large empty underground cavity in the mountain. The mountaintop, weakened by the eruption, sometimes collapses into the cavity.

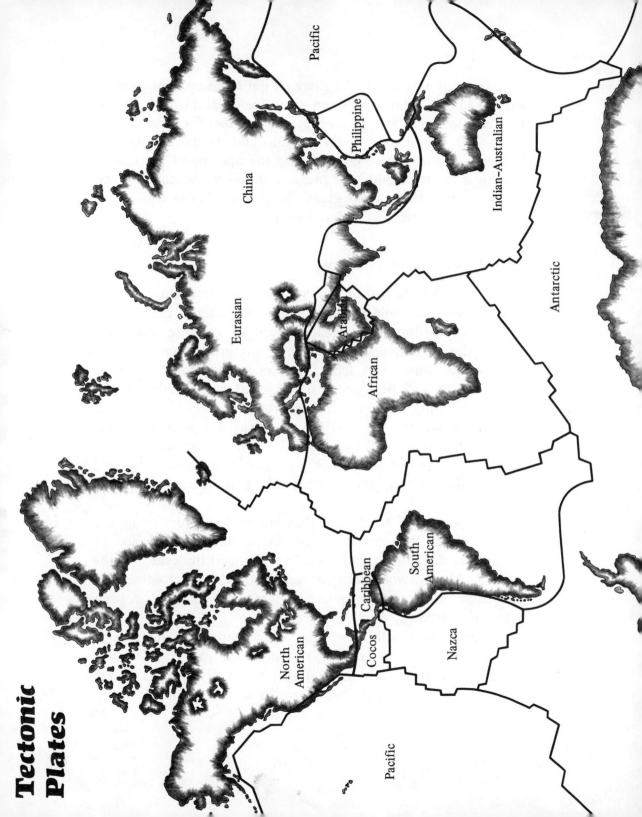

Tectonic Plates

Pacific

Philippine

China

Indian–Australian

Eurasian

Antarctic

Arabian

African

North American

Caribbean

South American

Cocos

Nazca

Pacific

In many volcanoes, the gases do not build up enough pressure to force the lava out in an explosive eruption. Instead, the lava just flows out through notches in the crater. The lava streams down over the outside of the volcano and, in time, cools and hardens. Cooling lava may also clog the opening of the crater, causing a further buildup of pressure inside the volcano. When the pressure becomes too great, the magma bursts out again, casting the plugged material into the air.

What Comes Out of Volcanoes

The molten magma that fuels volcanoes comes out as a combination of lava and volcanic gas. When the magma reaches the surface at the time of a volcanic eruption, pressure drops, allowing the magma and gases in the mixture to separate out. The way in which this separation occurs determines whether the explosion will be a gentle or a violent one, whether it will last several minutes or many hours.

Other factors, such as the chemical composition of the magma, the heat, and the pressure, also decide whether the magma appears as solid rock or as molten liquid lava and whether the pieces of rock blasted out of the volcano are small or large.

Fragments of solid rock that are hurled into the air are either magma that has hardened on reaching the surface or already hardened lava and rocks from around the crater of the volcano. Modern volcanologists, scientists who study volcanoes, call these solid rocks *pyroclastic* (pyro = fire, clastic = broken) material or *tephra*.

Tephra is usually new magmatic material that hardens as it is tossed out of the volcano's vent. If the particles are very small, less than 0.01 inches (0.03 cm) in diameter, they are *volcanic dust*; fragments between 0.01 and 0.15 inches (0.03

and 0.38 cm) are referred to as *ash*. Particles from 0.15 to 1.25 inches (0.38 to 3.18 cm) are called *lapilli,* from the Italian word for little stones. *Volcanic bombs* are smooth rocks of molten lava, greater than 1.25 inches (3.18 cm), which come out in a molten state and solidify when they make contact with the air; large-sized fragments that are solid when they erupt are known as *blocks*.

Often volcanoes do not toss lava up as tephra but push the lava out in thick, hot, runny streams that harden and eventually turn to rock. There are two main kinds of lava, both with Hawaiian names. Thick, frothy, slow-moving lava that becomes rough, jagged, and spiny when hardened and looks like stone rubble is called *aa* (pronounced ah-ah). The other type of lava, which is more liquid, less frothy, and faster moving is called *pahoehoe* (pa-hoyay-hoyay). As pahoehoe cools, it forms a thin, smooth skin that folds over as the still-liquid lava beneath it continues to flow, giving it the appearance of a thick twisted rope or cable.

Many volcanoes are located under water. The lava from these volcanoes is cooled immediately by the seawater and forms a hard skin over the still-molten interior. When these masses cool and harden, they appear very much like huge piles of pillows. For this reason they are named *pillow lava*.

Where Volcanoes Are Found

Volcanoes are found on every continent on earth except Australia. They are not, however, randomly scattered about. Rather, most volcanoes are found in a few well-defined zones. These zones are usually located near seacoasts in belts that follow the general outlines of some of the giant plates that make up the surface of the earth.

The giant Pacific plate is probably responsible for the

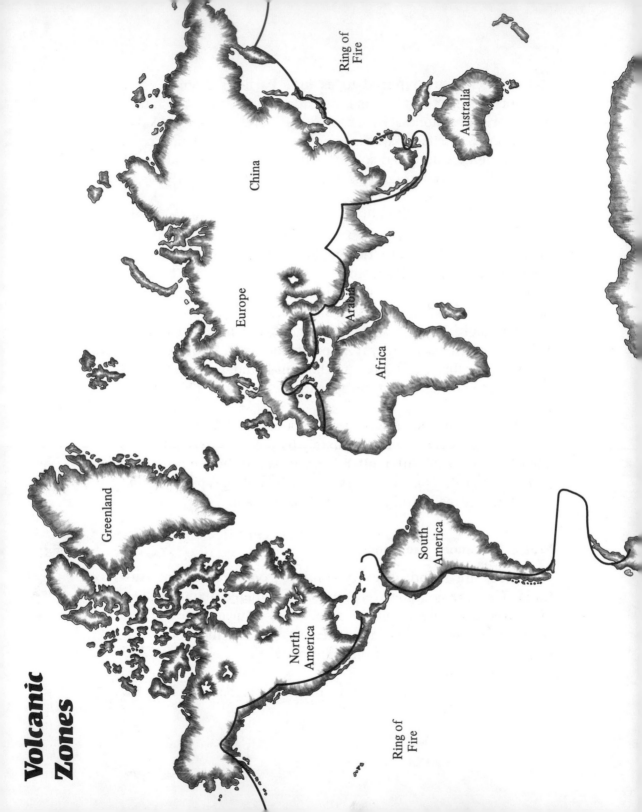

Volcanic Zones

Greenland

North America

South America

Ring of Fire

Ring of Fire

China

Europe

Arabia

Africa

Australia

greatest number of active volcanoes. This huge rock mass is pushing out against the western coasts of North and South America as well as against the eastern coast of Asia. As a result, the entire Pacific Ocean is encircled by a zone of volcanoes so distinctive that it is called the *Ring of Fire*.

This circular system includes the volcanoes along the west coasts of South, Central, and North America, the Aleutian Islands, the east coasts of Siberia, Japan, the Philippines, and Indonesia, through New Zealand and Antarctica and back to South America. Mount St. Helens in Washington State, Fujiyama (Mount Fuji) in Japan, and Krakatoa (also known as Krakatau) in Indonesia are three famous volcanoes in the Ring of Fire.

A number of well-known volcanoes in Italy result from the weaknesses along the line where the African plate and the Eurasian plate meet and bump up against one another. These volcanoes, which are located mostly around the Mediterranean Sea, take in Vesuvius, Etna, Stromboli, and Vulcano.

The volcanoes found on the Caribbean islands and some of those found in Central America are products of movements of the Caribbean and North American plates. Other, smaller zones of volcanic activity are caused by similar pressures on other plates.

While some plates are pushing against each other or sliding by each other, there are also plates that are pulling apart from each other. This, too, creates a volcanic zone. The best example of this is the Mid-Atlantic Ridge, along a north-south line that runs roughly up and down the middle of the Atlantic Ocean. The North American and Eurasian plates touch here and are very slowly pulling apart, so that there is volcanic activity along the length of the ridge.

Most of the volcanoes of the Mid-Atlantic Ridge are completely below sea level. These are called *sea mounts*. In a few places, though, they have broken through to the surface and formed islands, such as Iceland, the Azores, Ascension, and Tristan da Cunha. Ridges are also found in other oceans, and a certain number of volcanoes are found along these lines as well.

For some reason that is not yet fully understood, the group of volcanoes that make up the Hawaiian Islands is not found where two plates meet but rather near the middle of the immense Pacific plate. It is as though there is a permanent "hot spot" in the earth's crust at that point. The magma here apparently reaches the right combination of temperature and pressure to create a volcano.

Altogether about 1,000 volcanoes have been identified in the world today. Some 500 are considered active. That is, they have occasionally erupted within the last 25,000 years of human history. Every year an average of twenty to thirty of these active volcanoes erupt. The remaining volcanoes are either dormant, that is, they have not erupted for a very long period of time, but not so long that it is certain that they are dead; or they are extinct, which means they have been quiet throughout recorded history and will most likely never erupt again.

**Volcanoes: Forces of
Destruction and Construction**

Volcanoes are almost always thought of as bringers of death and destruction. Many people lose their lives as the result of volcanic eruptions. In the last 500 years alone, it is estimated that 200,000 people were killed by volcanoes.

Less well known, though, are the benefits that volcanoes bring. Volcanic deposits increase the land surfaces on which people can live. Hawaii and Iceland, for example, were formed by volcanoes. The material that falls to earth, although it may destroy plants, also contains many minerals, such as potassium, that add to the soil's fertility. The best coffee and tea in the world grow on the slopes of volcanoes, in soils enriched by volcanic debris. Valuable minerals, including gold, silver, and diamonds, and needed materials, such as copper, tin, tungsten, and sulphur, are brought to the surface during volcanic upheavals.

For those of us who have been spared the fear of living in the shadow of a volcano, such activity has created spectacular scenery that we may enjoy. We may also delight in photos, drawings, and other works of art inspired by the perfect shape and beauty of Fujiyama, the jagged landscape of Iceland, and the tropical lushness of Hawaii. Joseph M. Turner, the great British artist, produced some of his best paintings by capturing on canvas the brilliant sunsets and resplendent twilights caused by the great amounts of dust and ash released into the atmosphere by the 1815 eruption of Tambora. In our time, the volcanic dust cloud from Mount St. Helens changed the color of the evening sky and produced outstanding dawns and sunsets for many months.

To the scientist, volcanoes offer a special view into the earth's interior. In various parts of the world, scientists work in laboratories that rest on the slopes of active volcanoes. They are studying firsthand the way volcanoes behave. They are trying to understand better the conditions that trigger an eruption. What they learn is being used to predict volcanic activity and to help save lives and property.

3

Kinds of Volcanoes

No two volcanoes are exactly the same. Volcanoes differ in the type of magma they produce. They vary in the intensity of the eruptions. And each volcano forms a cone of a particular size and shape.

Varieties of Magma

The sort of magma that a volcano produces plays an important role in deciding the way it erupts. The main chemical elements in all magma are oxygen and silica, along with lesser amounts of iron, aluminum, potassium, calcium, magnesium, and others. The percentage of oxygen and silica determines the quality of the magma. Magma that is more than 66 percent oxygen and silica, combined into silicon dioxide, is said to be silica-rich. Such magma explodes out of the vent and produces lava that is thick and heavy, like molasses. Less than 50 percent silicon dioxide in the mix makes for silica-poor magma that pours out of the volcano and results in lava that is thin and souplike.

Rocks that form from silica-rich lava are called *rhyolites;* silica-poor lava yields *basalts*. Rocks that are between the two in chemical makeup are known as *andesites*.

The ease with which the gases dissolved in the magma escape also affects the way the volcano erupts. About two-thirds of the gas is steam; the remainder includes carbon monoxide, carbon dioxide, sulphur dioxide, and hydrogen sulfide. All of these gases come out at great heat; a number are deadly poisons. Gases that expand and escape easily as the magma rises to the surface produce quiet, gentle eruptions. Those that leave only with great difficulty give rise to violent, catastrophic explosions.

Volcanologists usually classify the many different types of eruptions into four broad groups: Hawaiian, Strombolian, Vulcanian, and Peléean. The names are taken from a well-known volcano of each type.

Not every eruption, however, fits neatly into one category or another. Many combine characteristics of two different types. Also, volcanoes frequently change, erupting in one way one time and then in a different way the next time. The following four types, though, can serve as a general guide to understanding the nature of volcanoes.

Hawaiian: Mild and Quiet

A Hawaiian-type eruption is one in which the silica-poor magma flows out of the volcano in nearly fluid form; it erupts with little violence. The lava flows readily from a central vent in what are sometimes called "rivers of fire." This kind of lava cools slowly, long after it emerges into the atmosphere.

Mauna Loa and Kilauea are two Hawaiian volcanoes that have these kinds of eruptions. Mauna Loa is the largest volcano in the world. It is over 30,000 feet (9,000 m) high, 17,000 feet (5,100 m) of which are below sea level. At ocean bottom it has a diameter of 124 miles (200 km). The volcano has been built up from about 10,000 cubic miles (44,000 cu km) of lava.

Icelandic volcanoes are very much like Hawaiian-type volcanoes in that they both pour out a fluidy, syrupy, silica-poor lava. The main difference is that while the Hawaiian type erupts through a central vent, the Icelandic variety usually pours out its lava through fissures or cracks in the earth's surface.

An Icelandic eruption creates no mountain on the surface of the earth. The lava spreads out very quickly and can cover thousands of square miles.

A series of such eruptions created the island of Iceland. Also, the Columbian Plateau in the northwestern United States, which covers 50,000 square miles (130,000 sq km) in the states of Washington, Oregon, and Idaho is the result of such eruptions ages ago. Scientists estimate that there are nearly 100,000 cubic miles (440,000 cu km) of basalt in this vast plain. India's Deccan Plain, which covers 100,000 square miles (260,000 sq km), was formed through similar deposits of thin, flowing basalt that bubbled up from the interior of the earth.

Strombolian:
Thicker Lava, Explosive

Strombolian eruptions produce somewhat denser lava than Hawaiian- or Icelandic-type volcanoes and release gases with more force and noise.

A typical Strombolian eruption takes place almost continuously, though usually with little flow of lava. From time to time, either at regular intervals or intermittently, gas escapes

In a Hawaiian-type eruption,
the lava is nearly all liquid
and flows out in hot streams.

from the lava, and there is a minor explosion. Observers report that it is like the noise of a jet engine at close range. Each explosion shoots blobs of lava into the air, most of which fall back into the crater itself. Only rarely is the explosion violent enough to send debris out over the surrounding area.

These kinds of eruptions take their name from the Stromboli volcano located in the Lipari Islands off the coast of Italy in the Mediterranean Sea. Stromboli has been exploding, almost without stop, for hundreds of years. Clouds of steam come up from three large vents in its crater, and glowing lava shoots up every fifteen to twenty minutes to heights of 500 to 1,000 feet (150 to 3,000 m) over the summit. The fiery-red light of the lava is reflected off the steam clouds and has been used by sailors as a beacon for many generations. This has earned Stromboli the title "Lighthouse of the Mediterranean."

Other Strombolian-type volcanoes are Mount Etna in nearby Sicily, Antarctica's Mount Erebus, and Pacaya in Guatemala, Central America.

Vulcanian or Vesuvian:
Tar-like Lava, Violent Explosion

Vulcanian eruptions are named after Vulcano, which is also found in the Lipari Islands off the coast of Italy. When such a volcano erupts, it produces very thick, silica-rich magma and explosions that are far more violent than those of a Strombolian volcano. Heavy clouds of volcanic gas, dust, and ash rise from the powerful outbursts that accompany each eruption.

Although explosive activity does not occur very often in Vulcanian-type volcanoes, it may go on for months at a time when it does take place. Irazu, the Vulcanian volcano in Costa Rica, was actively erupting from 1963 to 1965.

Vesuvian eruptions are similar to Vulcanian but more

—20

forceful. The powerful explosions form large clouds of gas and dust that shoot up high into the air, spreading ash over wide areas. Vesuvian volcanoes usually erupt with one sustained blast. Vulcanian eruptions, on the other hand, produce occasional blasts over days or months.

The well-known Mount Vesuvius volcano in Italy has averaged about one major explosion every twenty-five to thirty years. During the eruption of Vesuvius in A.D. 79, the blast buried the city of Pompeii, about 5 miles (8 km) from the volcano, in over 10 feet (3 m) of dust and ash.

Peléean: Thick Lava, Gigantic Explosion, Glowing Cloud

The Peléean is the most violent of all volcanic eruptions. It is characterized by the formation of a superhot, glowing cloud of gas and molten lava, a *nuée ardente* that shoots out of the top or side of the volcano after an immensely powerful explosion.

A nuée ardente is made up of a mass of red-hot solid rock fragments that are lifted high by the rush of expanding, heated gases. The immensely hot and powerful nuée ardente advances at hurricane-wind speeds over the ground, destroying everything in its path. Neither buildings, plants, people, nor animals can survive this onslaught.

Peléean volcanoes are named after Mont Pelée on the island of Martinique in the Caribbean Sea. Mount Lamington in Papua and a number of volcanoes in the Philippines are among other examples of Peléean volcanoes.

Shapes of Volcanoes

When a volcano erupts and spews out lava, most of the lava collects and eventually hardens around the opening, usually form-

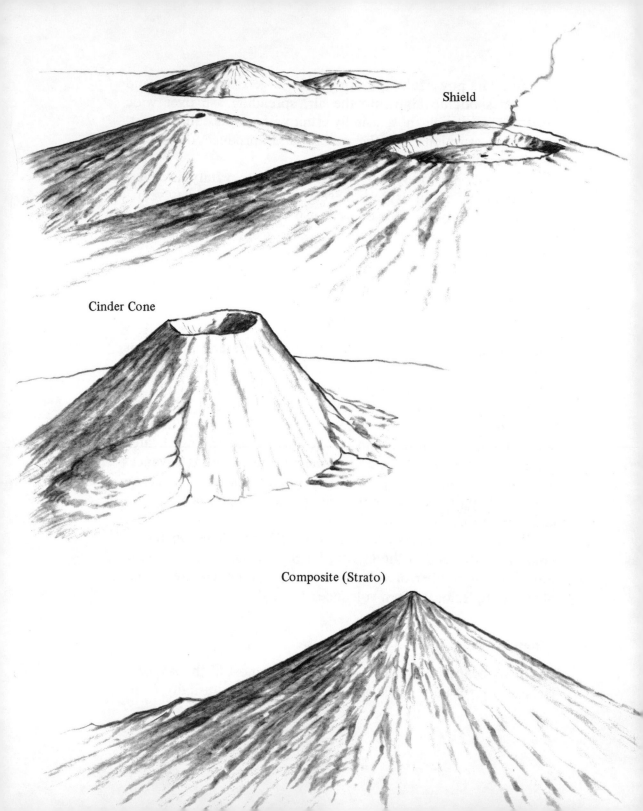

Shield

Cinder Cone

Composite (Strato)

ing a well-shaped cone. The exact outline, though, depends on the makeup of the magma in its interior and the way it erupts.

Shield volcanoes are named after the slightly curved shields used by ancient warriors. They are shaped like upturned saucers, with very gentle slopes. These volcanoes are built up of many successive outflows of basaltic fluid lava from a central vent, such as occurs in Hawaiian-type eruptions.

As the lava flows out, more remains near the vent than travels away. The volcano, therefore, has an outcropping of lava around the opening, with a gradual flattening out away from the vent. Shield volcanoes usually have very broad bases with sides that seldom slope at angles greater than 10°. They can become very high mountains. The Hawaiian volcanoes, Mauna Loa and Kilauea, are outstanding examples of shield volcanoes.

Cinder cone volcanoes, consisting of ash and other solid fragments, are commonly found where the eruptions produce mostly tephra. The fragments fall on all sides of the opening, creating a cone around the vent and forming steep slopes. Eruptions of these kinds of volcanoes produce little lava. Typical cinder cone volcanoes, such as Paricutin in Mexico, Sunset Crater in Arizona, and Mono and Amboy in California, have bases no more than about 1 mile (1.6 km) in diameter and steep sides up to an angle of 35°. They reach heights of no more than 1,500 feet (450 m).

The *composite* or *strato volcanoes* fall somewhere between the shield and cinder cone in shape. They are steeper than the shield volcanoes and often more symmetrical than the cinder cones. Their slopes, at angles between 20° and 30°, are formed by the buildup of alternating layers of molten lava, like shield volcanoes, and tephra, like cinder cones.

A typical composite volcano may start with an eruption that deposits a layer of tephra around the vent. The next eruption is an outflow of lava that pours out over the rocks. The pileup of

*Above: Mauna Loa, the largest volcano
in the world, is a shield volcano. It has
a number of craters on its surface and
a 3-mile (4.8-km) caldera at its summit.
Right: Cerro Negro volcano in Nicaragua
has a cinder cone shape.*

alternating layers, one on top of the other, produces the most attractive-looking, picture postcard-type volcanoes, such as the spectacular Fujiyama of Japan, Italy's Mount Vesuvius, and Mounts Rainier, Hood, and Shasta in the United States.

Craters and Calderas

Most volcanoes have openings at their summits called *craters,* through which the lava and gases emerge. These funnel-shaped depressions are commonly formed by the explosive force of the eruption and the piling up of debris around the vent. Ordinary craters range from a few feet (.6 m) to 1 mile (1.6 km) across and may be as much as 2,000 feet (600 m) deep.

Extremely large craters, more than 1 mile (1.6 km) in diameter, are called *calderas,* from the Spanish word for kettle. Calderas are formed either by a tremendously powerful explosion or by the collapse of the summit into an underground cavity.

Calderas are especially common on old volcanoes. Lakes often form in them from rainwater and melted snow. Crater Lake atop Mount Mazama in the Cascade Mountains of Oregon is one such body of water. It measures 6 miles (10 km) by 4 miles (6.4 km) and is nearly 2,000 feet (600 m) deep. The sides of the lake tower another 2,000 feet (600 m) over the level of the water. Scientists believe that Crater Lake was created by an eruption of Mount Mazama about 6,600 years ago. Wizard Island, an outcropping in the middle of Crater Lake, is the cone of a newly active volcano within the caldera of Mount Mazama.

Probably the largest caldera on earth is found on the Asosan volcano in Japan. It measures about 14.3 by 10 miles (23 by 16 km). Even larger is one caldera observed on the planet Mars. Olympus Mons, a shield volcano with a 372-mile (600-km) diameter, has a caldera that is 50 miles (80 km) wide.

4

Paricutin, 1943-1952: Birth and Death of a Volcano

Paricutin in Mexico is the newest volcano to form in the Western hemisphere. Volcanologists consider Paricutin an ordinary cinder cone volcano in most respects. What makes it special is that Paricutin is the first volcano that scientists have observed from its moment of birth in 1943, through the nine years of its active life, to its probable death, or extinction, in 1952.

Birth of the Volcano

Paricutin began as a hole in the ground. A very old woman in the Mexican village of Paricutin, about 180 miles (300 km) west of Mexico City, later remembered the spot. It was just 2 miles (3.2 km) outside of her village. She had played there as a child. She especially remembered the feel of warm soil under her bare feet and the deep rumbling sounds that came from the ground below.

Around 1940, a hole appeared in the middle of Dionisio

—27

Pulido's nine-acre farm. Several times Pulido tried to fill the hole with soil, but after a few months, the opening in the earth would be back again.

On February 5, 1943, the residents of the area felt a series of mild earthquakes near Paricutin. Since this part of Mexico has frequent earthquakes, no one was alarmed by the slight tremors. Although Pulido also noticed the earth tremors, he had no reason to associate them with the strange hole in his cornfield that he could never fill in. He just went ahead with his plans for spring plowing and planting.

Just after noon on February 20, as Dionisio and a hired worker, Demetrio Toral, were clearing the old growth off the land, they heard loud rumbling noises coming from the ground. Dionisio compared it to "a noise like thunder during a rainstorm." But since it was a clear, peaceful day, they just kept on working.

When they got ready to burn off the pile of brush they had collected, they noticed that the old hole in the field had become a crack about 20 inches (50 cm) deep. Although it seemed peculiar, the farmers kept working until about four o'clock, at which time the whole earth began to tremble violently beneath them.

To their amazement, the land around the crack began to bulge and rise, reaching up to 8 feet (2.4 m) above the surface. And then with a hissing, whistling sound, a column of fine, gray dust rose up from out of the ground, and sulphur gas and steam began to ooze out of the crack. Terrified, the men fled to their homes in the village.

Word of the strange happenings in the cornfield spread to the nearby town of San Juan de Parangaricutiro. A party of volunteers, after receiving the blessing of the priest, were sent to investigate the matter at close range. One man, who tried to look into the fuming hole, stepped too near the edge and almost fell in as a ridge of soil gave way.

The "hole" was now a pit that measured nearly 6 feet (1.8 m) across. Small explosions were tossing gray smoke, ashes, and red-hot stones up from the earth, some to a height of 15 feet (4.5 m). Within hours, the ash and stones had formed a mound around the crack about 20 inches (50 cm) high.

Farmers came from miles around that night to observe the erupting, glowing rocks—"sparks" they called them—and the ever-growing cloud of ash that reached some 2,500 feet (750 m) above Dionisio's field. By morning, where the villagers expected to see a big fissure, there was instead a 30-foot (9-m)-high cone of ash and rock.

Someone realized that what he was witnessing was the birth of a volcano and notified the authorities. A number of scientists arrived on the scene. They began making careful observations and keeping detailed records on the volcano's growth and development.

Within a few days the growing volcano, already named Volcáno de Parícutin, became more violent and active. Powerful explosions cast great blobs of burning lava 3,000 feet (900 m) into the atmosphere. Rivers of fire flowed down the sides of the volcano. By the end of February, the solidified lava and rocks had created a volcano 500 feet (150 m) high. Explosive sounds were heard as far away as Mexico City, nearly 200 miles (320 km) to the east. The inhabitants of Paricutin were forced to begin abandoning their homes and farms.

The very young volcano kept changing its character. After a while it stopped emitting lava and rock and began to spit out giant clouds of volcanic dust and ash. Some of these clouds reached heights of 20,000 feet (6,000 m). But before very long the material that came up from the volcano changed again, and lava began to flow from its crater.

Not yet one year old, the volcano was already about 1,200 feet (360 m) high and more than half a mile (800 m) across. Then, at the beginning of the new year, 1944, still another type of eruption occurred. Instead of forcing its way up to the crater, the lava now began to pour out through fissures in the side of the cone. First one fissure opened and then another, under the relentless pressure of the rising magma.

Pools of lava formed and flowed down to lower ground. One particularly heavy stream, in September 1944, traveled 5 miles (8 km). The lava was very thick and heavy and moved very slowly. Scientists flying over the area estimated the flow at approximately 100 feet (30 m) per hour.

The slow-spreading sea of lava eventually came to cover 7 square miles (17 sq km) of land. Though the residents had all been evacuated in time and there was no loss of life, the entire village of Paricutin and the larger town, San Juan, were completely buried under successive layers of lava and destroyed for all time. The lava flowed in, around, and over everything that lay in its path. Of the entire town of San Juan, all that was left poking up above the solid block of lava was the top of the church steeple.

As it turned out, the year 1943 was Paricutin's heaviest period of activity. The volcano rose from a height of 120 feet (36 m) at the end of the first day to a mountain 1,200 feet

Sometimes Paricutin emitted giant clouds of dust and ash. Other times it flung up lava and rock.

(360 m) tall by the end of the year. Even though it did contain some lava, it was essentially a cinder cone volcano.

Maturity

By the time the second year had passed, Paricutin had reached a maximum height of about 1,600 feet (500 m) and a diameter at its base of 1 mile (1.6 km). Although explosions continued for the next few years of its life, none of this activity added to its size.

The general pattern of eruptions remained the same for the next few years. Explosions still flung tephra, from fine dust to blocks weighing many tons, up through the crater and into the atmosphere. At other times, lava would ooze and flow from fissures in the sides of the volcano. The amount of ash produced, however, declined greatly over the years, as did the amounts of lava, though at a much slower rate.

Despite a continued decline in activity, Paricutin erupted until March 4, 1952, when, after a little more than nine years of explosions, all activity suddenly ceased, and the volcano became quiet. Most volcanologists believe that volcanoes such as Paricutin erupt over a period of time and then die or become extinct. A dome of hardened lava covers the vent, and the conduit is filled with a plug, called a *spine,* of solid rock.

Soon after the volcano stopped erupting, volcanologists from many countries, who had come to Mexico to observe the volcano, packed their bags and left for home. What they left behind, though, was a thorough biography of Paricutin. One scientist, Carl Fries, Jr., guessed that 3,700 tons (3,360 m.t.) of tephra and lava were ejected over the volcano's nine-year life. In just the year 1945, he estimated, the volcano vented the equivalent of 14,330 tons (13,000 m.t.) of water daily.

Today, the summit of the volcano is 1,345 feet (410 m) above its base. The slopes of the cone are at a 33° angle, and the crater is very large compared to the width of the cone. Gradually the crater will become filled with loose debris falling into it from the walls. Its profile, though it will grow a little less sharp, will probably remain unchanged for a very long time to come.

5

Vesuvius, A.D. 79: The Destruction of Pompeii

Vesuvius, probably the most famous volcano in the world, is also the only active volcano on the mainland of Europe. It is located about 6 miles (10 km) southeast of the city of Naples, in one of the most populated parts of Italy. Its fame is due largely to its frequent eruptions, which occur roughly every twenty-five to thirty years. During an eruption a great column of dust and ash rises up over Naples and reaches many miles into the atmosphere.

Vesuvius' history of disastrous eruptions spans some 12,000 years. The last eruption was in March 1944. Despite the devastating consequences of its volcanic activity over the centuries, families continue to live on the slopes and around the foot of the mountain. Like their ancestors, the people there still grow crops in its very fertile soil and harvest the grapes of their vineyards.

Pompeii and Herculaneum

While there is reason to believe that Vesuvius erupted in prehistoric as well as later times, there is no written account of it hap-

*The eruption of Mount Vesuvius
in March, 1944. Note the giant
pine-tree shape of its cloud.*

pening before A.D. 79. At that time, there was apparently a sudden and violent eruption of the volcano, which killed thousands of people and annihilated the cities of Pompeii and Herculaneum. Most of what we know of this eruption is through the writings of the Roman author Pliny the Younger, who was seventeen at the time of the devastation.

Until A.D. 79, the Romans had considered Vesuvius to be extinct. Violent earthquakes shook the area from time to time, but no one took it as a sign of an impending eruption, as people do today. The sudden appearance of an immense black cloud arising out of Vesuvius on the morning of August 24, in the year A.D. 79, caught everyone by surprise.

Many thousands of people lived in the prosperous towns and ports around the Bay of Naples, including the well-known naturalist Pliny the Elder. Curious to learn more about the eruption, he approached the volcano by boat, stopping to rescue a friend on the way. The effort cost him his life. Later, the historian Tacitus asked Pliny the Younger to describe the circumstances of his uncle's death and to give an account of the eruption in general. Pliny's two letters to Tacitus provide many details on events that took place when the volcano erupted just over 1,900 years ago.

Apparently the strange cloud seen over the volcano at first seemed harmless. As it rose higher, however, it became more menacing. People became fearful as the huge mass of dust spread upward and out, until it resembled a gigantic pine tree. Soon hot ash and stones from the eruption started to rain down on the city. Poisonous gas and fumes filled the air. By evening the heavy ash cloud glowed red from the molten lava and the many fires started by the hot ash. Tremors shook the houses. By the next morning, a dense pall of dust and ash from the volcano blocked out the sun.

Those who took refuge in homes were killed by the hot ash or by roofs that collapsed under the weight of the ash pileup. Many others breathed in the poisonous air and died from suffocation caused by the sulphurous fumes of the ash cloud.

The dead or dying were soon covered over by the falling ash. The rains that followed cemented all the ash together into a solid, hard mass around the corpses, making nearly perfect molds of the bodies where they fell. These molds, and the casts that were later made from them, show the agony on the faces of the suffocation victims, many of whom died clutching at their throats. It is estimated that about 15,000 men, women, and children died in this way.

Among those who fled the city were Pliny the Younger and his mother. Along with many other refugees they headed for open country. Flashes of lightning flickered across the sky as the ash cloud discharged bursts of electricity. Even in the open fields, people were overwhelmed by dense ash clouds that turned day into night. The ash piled up all around. From time to time those fleeing had to shake themselves off so they wouldn't be buried alive.

The eruption lasted for two terrible days. At the end of this time, a pale daylight peeked through the heavy haze of dust. Tons of hot, wet stones and ash were piled up on the streets of Pompeii. The city was almost entirely covered over. Returning survivors could find no trace of homes, relatives, or belongings. Eventually they gave up searching for remains and abandoned the city altogether.

The lesser known town of Herculaneum, to the west of Vesuvius, was smaller—5,000 inhabitants at most, compared with the 25,000 of Pompeii—and lower on the slope of Vesuvius. Herculaneum did not get the immense fallout of volcanic dust that destroyed Pompeii. Instead, it was devastated by a flow of

*When Vesuvius erupts,
crackling static electricity
can be seen in the sky.*

volcanic mud formed from ash that had fallen on the slopes of the volcano and been wet down by heavy rains. A wall of mud came crashing down the mountain toward Herculaneum, covering the town and harbor to a height of 60 feet (18 m). Eventually, it dried and hardened into a solid cementlike rock, leaving no trace of the city.

The great eruption of A.D. 79 is remembered principally for having obliterated the cities of Pompeii and Herculaneum. But the ashfall and mudslides did more than that. They changed the whole region around Naples, altering the course of rivers and raising the coast. The smooth cone of Vesuvius blew away or collapsed, and a huge crater, Monte Somma, was formed on the north side. Fields and vineyards, and miles of rolling countryside, were buried or leveled. No animals, birds, or insects were left alive.

Excavation of the Ruins

For over 1,500 years after the A.D. 79 eruption, the sites of the two ancient cities were largely forgotten and untouched. Around 1600, workmen digging a canal for an aqueduct unearthed some coins and jewelry around the site of Pompeii, but no effort was made to uncover the city. It was not until 1748, when a peasant digging in a vineyard struck a buried wall and brought it to the attention of government officials, that plans to excavate were first made.

The digging to recover the valuables buried in the volcanic material went on for about a hundred years. Then, after 1860, a new director of excavations decided to uncover the whole city, street by street, according to a carefully worked out plan. Scientists continue to work to restore Pompeii to its original condition.

Today you can see much of the unearthed city of Pompeii almost as it looked in A.D. 79, despite an earthquake in November 1980 that destroyed part of the excavated ruins. You can walk up and down the narrow lanes and look into the shops and houses that line the street. You can see what life in Pompeii was like 1,900 years ago. Food, clothes, buildings, statues, and mosaics that were freed from the rock are on display.

Excavations at Herculaneum were hampered by the fact that the modern city of Resina is built on the exact same site. Scientists had to use a system of shafts and tunnels to reach the buried areas. The mud that had covered Herculaneum had hardened into a much stronger and denser material than at Pompeii, making it much more difficult to penetrate. In addition, the buildings and objects that have been found are of less interest than those from Pompeii because the flowing mud damaged them to a great degree.

Since the remains of only fifteen bodies were originally found at Herculaneum, it had long been assumed that the mud flow had moved towards the city slowly, giving the populace plenty of time to flee. The discovery of another four bodies during the summer of 1980 is now leading some scientists to believe that the mud may have advanced much faster than had been thought, and that many more people were killed as they tried to escape the rushing avalanche. Ongoing excavations may soon reveal how many people actually perished in the destruction of Herculaneum.

Later Eruptions

After the eruption of A.D. 79, Vesuvius remained quiet for nearly a hundred years. The year A.D 172, however, started a series of some forty eruptions that have taken place over the years since. The eruptions, some major, some minor, have built up a new volcanic cone, Gran Cono, on the south side.

Records show that in 472, great clouds of volcanic ash poured from the crater and were blown as far as Constantinople (Istanbul), Turkey, by the winds. Streams of lava poured out and flowed down the mountain in 1631, killing about 18,000 people.

During the eighteenth and nineteenth centuries, destructive eruptions of Vesuvius occurred in 1794, 1822, 1855, 1872, 1880, and 1895. After each eruption, farmers would return to the mountainside to rebuild their homes and cultivate the land. In 1872, twenty-two sightseers were killed when they went up Mount Vesuvius to watch streams of lava advancing and became caught between two of them.

In 1906, a major eruption eradicated several towns. It also claimed many lives, including those of a frightened group of villagers in San Giuseppe who assembled in the local church thinking they would be safe there. When the roof of the church collapsed under the weight of the heavy ash, almost all were killed. Had they remained at home shoveling the ash from their roofs, they might have been saved.

Before Vesuvius last erupted, in March 1944, hordes of tourists came to the mountain each year. A cable railway, destroyed in the 1944 explosions, took visitors to within 450 feet (135 m) of the edge of the crater. People could climb down into the crater and observe the flow of molten lava cooling and turning to stone.

Most volcanologists believe that another eruption of Vesuvius is inevitable. An eruption in modern times, though, would cause greater loss of life and devastation than at any other time in history, because of the large increase in population over the last forty years. The scientists are watching Vesuvius very closely to try to predict when it will erupt again.

6

Krakatoa, 1883: The Volcano Heard Halfway Around the World

The arc of islands that make up the nation of Indonesia include some of the world's most active and powerful volcanoes. The eruption of one of these island volcanoes, in August 1883, caused the greatest volcanic disaster in recorded history.

Much of the island was blown to pieces. Some 5 cubic miles (20 cu km) of rock, ash, and dust were flung into the air. Volcanic dust and debris floated around the region for about one year. The roar of the explosion was heard halfway around the world, and huge waves caused by the shock washed over nearby islands, killing more than 36,000 people.

History of Krakatoa

A small island about 5½ miles (9 km) long, Krakatoa lay in the Sunda Straits, a narrow body of water between the two large islands of Java and Sumatra. Geologists say that nearly one million years ago in that spot there had been a giant volcano that had been blown apart, leaving only one large island plus Krakatoa and a number of smaller islands above the surface of the sea. On Krakatoa there was a north-south line of volcanic cones. The northernmost was called Perboewetan; the southernmost, and largest, was Rakata.

The earliest recorded eruption of Krakatoa took place between May 1680 and November 1681. Little is known of this incident. Reports just told that all of the lush vegetation on the island was destroyed, and that large quantities of rock fell into the sea. Being filled with gas bubbles, the rocks were light enough to float about in the Sunda Straits.

In time, the plant growth returned to the island, and Krakatoa again became covered with a thick tropical forest. It remained uninhabited, though. The only visitors to the island were occasional sightseers and woodcutters, who chopped down some of the larger trees for markets in Java or Sumatra.

Onset of the Catastrophe

The first hint that something was brewing on Krakatoa came on September 1, 1880, when a particularly strong earthquake hit the area. The quakes continued over the following months, increasing in intensity until May 20, 1883, when the volcano suddenly came to life. A loud series of explosions could be heard up to nearly 100 miles (160 km) away. Also, coming from within the earth, a tall column of steam and ash rose, reaching, according to observers, a height of 7 miles (11 km) above the summit.

Within a week, the activity had quieted down enough for a boatload of sightseers to sail to the island, where a party even ventured ashore. The noise was still deafening. One of the onlookers said that in all the din a rifle shot sounded as loud as "the popping of a champagne cork amid the hubbub of a banquet."

As they waded through the white, ankle-deep volcanic dust, the observers in the group saw that most of the volcanic activity was centered in Perboewetan. Explosions continued every five or ten minutes, with a column of steam rising nearly 2 miles (3.2 km) into the sky. The more foolhardy visitors went to the rim of the crater and found it to be about 3,300 feet (1,000 m) across and 164 feet (50 m) deep, with a small pit in the middle of the crater floor from which steam was boiling up.

The volcano continued to be very active for another week or two and then grew quiet. On June 19, it started to get more agitated. A second column of steam was seen rising from closer to the center of the island. More explosions, outpourings of steam and ash, and earthquakes followed. On August 11, a government official sailed close to the island and reported three vents in active eruption, with at least eleven others ejecting smaller columns of steam and occasional puffs of ash and dust.

Over the next two weeks the volcanoes grew ever more restless and violent. By one o'clock on the afternoon of August 26, explosions were coming about every ten minutes. One hour later, sailors on a ship 75 miles (120 km) away could see a black cloud rising to 16 miles (25 km) above the island. Soon, shocks were heard and felt up to 100 miles (160 km) distant, and there was a heavy fall of large pieces of rock all over the area.

As it grew dark, Krakatoa began to look like an inferno. The great dark cloud over the volcano took on the giant pine-tree shape. It glowed red from the heat of the molten lava. Fierce bolts of lightning flashed through the cloud. The explosions were coming with such frequency that they sounded like one continuous roar. And the rain of hot ash along with the choking fumes of the gases turned the scene into a vision of horror. Still, the worst was yet to come.

Climactic Explosions

With the coming of dawn on Monday, August 27, 1883, four immense explosions—at 5:30, 6:44, 10:02, and 10:52 A.M.—completely ripped apart the entire island. The strongest one, which occurred at 10:02, was probably the biggest explosion, natural or man-made, ever to occur in the history of the earth.

The power of these blasts was so strong that walls cracked and windows were shattered up to 100 miles (160 km) away. In Australia, some 2,000 miles (3,200 km) away, people were awakened by the boom. The farthest point where the detonation was heard was at Rodriguez Island in the Indian Ocean, a full 3,000 miles (4,800 km) from the volcano!

During that morning, some two-thirds of the entire island disappeared. The volcanic material and gases formed an enormous cloud that reached some 50 miles (80 km) above the surface of the earth. According to eyewitness reports, what came down ranged from dust and ash to blocks as large as pumpkins. Giant rafts of light volcanic rock collected in the waters around Krakatoa, some reaching 10 feet (3 m) in length. These rafts made the movement of ships in the area very difficult for a long time to come.

Since no one lived on Krakatoa, the eruption itself took no lives. The 36,000 people whose deaths are blamed on the volcano were killed by giant waves, called tsunamis, unleashed by the fury of the eruption. The tsunamis rushed out from Krakatoa in all directions. At first the waves were only a few feet

*The 1883 eruption of Krakatoa
was probably the most powerful
explosion in recorded history.
It was re-created in the film
Krakatoa, East of Java,
from which this photo comes.*

tall. But as they raced toward the coasts of Java and Sumatra they reached heights of about 125 feet (38 m), about as high as a twelve-story building. Nearly 300 towns and villages in coastal areas were smashed and washed out to sea.

The waves kept on their murderous path all day, spreading through the oceans at about 400 miles (640 km) per hour. The following morning abnormally high water levels were noticed as far away as the English Channel, along the coast of Panama, and even in San Francisco, where the water rose 6 inches (15 cm) above normal.

The powerful volcanic activity at Krakatoa continued until about eleven that night, when the ferocity of the eruption began to decline. At about 2:30 on the afternoon of the next day, the entire eruption was over. A survey team went out to the island, or rather to what was left of the island.

The entire northern part of Krakatoa was gone. The volcano Perboewetan and the line of other smaller volcanoes had disappeared. And of the large Rakata volcano, only the southern part of the cone remained. Where the island had stood nearly 1,000 feet (300 m) above sea level, there was now a vast underwater crater, about 1,000 feet (300 m) down.

The fine dust thrown high up into the atmosphere by the eruption was spread out over the entire world by the winds. As a result, there were many reports of especially brilliant, bright-red sunsets for a period of two years, and even a few reports of the sun appearing green or other colors. The climate also changed; it grew cooler because the warming sunlight could not come through.

Child of Krakatoa

The story of Krakatoa did not end with the eruption of 1883. Rumblings from deep within the earth and minor quakes kept on throughout the following decades. On January 25, 1925, a small volcanic cone peeked above the water that was covering the island. Gradually it grew taller and larger. Then, in October 1952, an eruption raised it to a height of 200 feet (60 m). Other eruptions continued to add lava and rock to the cone. Today, it is well over 300 feet (90 m) above sea level. This newly formed volcano is called Anak Krakatoa, which means "child of Krakatoa." The remarkable island volcano may not be dead after all.

7

Mont Pelée, 1902:
The Cloud of Death

The first recorded eruption of Mont Pelée, a small, 4,430-foot (1,350-m) volcano on the northern end of the tropical island of Martinique in the Caribbean Sea, took place in 1727. In 1767 and 1772 mild earthquakes struck the island, but life in St. Pierre, the largest city on Martinique and often called the "Paris of the Caribbean," was hardly affected at all.

In 1851 the underground temperature of Mont Pelée had risen so high, the lake that had formed in the smaller of two craters evaporated, and the crater became a dry bed. Some minor eruptions followed, spreading a fine layer of volcanic dust over the city, about 6 miles (9.6 km) to the southwest of the volcano.

For the remainder of the century the volcano was peaceful, and people stopped worrying about it. Little did they know that before much longer the entire city of St. Pierre, and its 34,000 inhabitants, would be erased from the face of the earth.

Diary of an Eruption

• *April 23, 1902.* A series of mild earthquakes strike the area, just strong enough to rattle some dishes and crack some walls in St. Pierre. Three loud explosions are heard, seemingly from within the mountain.

• *April 25, 1902.* The volcano begins to emit ash and gas. Animals are dying in the streets of St. Pierre, suffocated by the poisonous gases.

• *April 27, 1902.* Some observers go up the side of the volcano. They find that the small crater, dry since 1851, is now a lake filled with water. Meanwhile the fall of ash goes on, coating everything and everybody with an increasingly thick layer of fine, gray dust. People, unable to breathe, sickened by the smell, and suffering from sore throats and irritated eyes, remain inside their houses behind closed doors and sealed windows. More animals, unable to avoid the clinging dust and acrid gases, are becoming sick and dying.

• *May 2, 1902. 11:30* A.M. An explosion on Mont Pelée unleashes a giant cloud of steam and great amounts of ash and rock into the air. Tremendous bolts of lightning flash up from the small crater, the center of the eruption. The entire northern half of the island of Martinique disappears under a coating of ash, as though a freak snowstorm had just passed over the island. Stores and schools close as life in St. Pierre comes to a halt. The few who venture out move silently through the deserted streets, their footsteps muffled by the thick layer of dust and ash. The dust particles in the air and the moisture produce a torrential rainfall. The level of water in the crater lake grows higher and higher. The temperature of the water also rises, so high that the water begins to boil!

—50

• *May 5, 1902. 12:30* P.M. Suddenly, the side of the crater lake gives way. With a thunderous roar, the hot water, now mixed with volcanic ash to form a thin mud, begins sliding down the side of the mountain. Traveling at a speed of about a mile (1.6 km) a minute, the half-mile (0.8-km)-wide flow races along, destroying everything in its path and claiming many human victims.

• *May 5, 1902. 12:33* P.M. The avalanche of mud now reaches the sea, 3 miles (4.8 km) from the volcano. A sugar mill stands at this point. In an instant the boiling mud spreads all over the mill, killing the forty workers inside. All that remains visible are the factory's tall smokestacks. Farmers and villagers from the outlying districts rush to St. Pierre for refuge. Many of the citizens of St. Pierre, though, are trying to flee. But they are being stopped by soldiers posted along the various roads. The reason? Louis Mouttet, the governor of Martinique, wants to make sure that the people remain in the city to vote for him in the upcoming election!

• *May 8, 1902. 7:52* A.M. A bright, clear morning, Ascension Day, and the church bells are loudly chiming. A tall column of steam and ash is rising above Mont Pelée, but by now everyone is used to that. All at once, four loud reports ring out from the volcano. "It was like a thousand cannons," a sailor on one of the ships in the harbor later wrote.

• *May 8, 1902. 7:59* A.M. The side of the mountain explodes. An immense, glowing cloud of superhot steam, molten lava, and giant boulders bursts out of the crater at a speed estimated at 300 miles (480 km) per hour—and it is aimed directly at St. Pierre! The hurricane force of the glowing cloud, a nuée ardente, levels everything in its path. The rapidly moving surge of hot gas, believed to be about 1,800° F (1,000° C), melts glass, twists the heaviest steel beams, and instantly turns wood into charcoal. Anyone who gasps for a breath of air perishes immediately, the heat completely shriveling the lungs.

While the cloud hangs over the city, there are no fires, since there is not enough oxygen to feed the flames. But as soon as the cloud is gone, the air rushes in and fires burst out all over, burning to a crisp anything that still remains.

May 8, 1902. 8:02 A.M. The cloud is completely gone. The hands on the big clock atop the military hospital mark the exact moment when the holocaust ended—only three minutes after it began. Within those three minutes, though, 34,000 people were killed by the fury of the volcano, and an entire city was reduced to rubble.

Only two people survived the disaster. One was a twenty-eight-year-old shoemaker, Léon Compère-Leandre, whose house somehow escaped the full fury of the eruption. "I was seated on the doorstep of my house," he wrote. "All of a sudden I felt a terrible wind blowing, the earth began to tremble, and the sky suddenly became dark. I turned to go into the house . . . and felt my arms and legs burning, also my body. Crazed and almost overcome, I threw myself upon a bed, inert and awaiting death. My senses returned to me in about an hour, when I beheld the roof burning."

No one can guess how Compère-Leandre managed to live through those awful few minutes while everyone else was consumed by the heat and flames. Though badly burned, he was able to get to the next village, where he received help.

The other man to escape death was a convicted murderer, Auguste Ciparis, twenty-five years old and a former dock worker. Ciparis was being held prisoner in the city's dungeon, awaiting hanging. His cell was cramped and dark, with thick, heavy walls. It had a tiny, solid door only 2 feet (.06 m) high and a small grated window over the door for ventilation.

In his isolated room, Ciparis had no idea of what was happening until he felt a blast of heat force its way in through the small opening. His back and legs were badly burned, but, as with Compère-Leandre, it did not kill him.

Ciparis remained confined for four days, in terrible pain from his infected burns and without food or water. Finally a rescue team from a neighboring town freed him. While he was left with permanent scars, he recovered from his ordeal and was subsequently pardoned. The ex-convict spent the remaining twenty-seven years of his life in circus sideshows, exhibiting his mutilated body in a reconstruction of his cell. He went under the billing, "The Prisoner of St. Pierre."

The eruption of May 8 did not completely exhaust Mont Pelée. It exploded again on May 20. The few people who had returned to St. Pierre in the hope of starting anew, and the few buildings that were left standing, were all destroyed by the new blast.

Over the following months, there were many more eruptions of red-hot lava and clouds of hot gas, although with less violence. The fury of the volcano appeared to be spent. Mont Pelée remained dormant until August 1929, when an earthquake and the sounds of explosions within the mountain again signaled an impending eruption. This time everyone heeded the warning and evacuated the city. When the eruption did come, on September 16, it was not a serious one and caused only some minor property damage, without any loss of life.

The final phase of the eruption of Mont Pelée was the growth of a lava dome in the summit crater and a solid spine of lava in the conduit. Thus Mont Pelée is repeating the same pattern of many volcanoes. It is a cycle that begins with an eruption of gas and ash and ends with a dome and spine when the gas and magma are spent.

8

Mount St. Helens, 1980: Volcanologists at Work

The eruption of Mount St. Helens in the spring of 1980 was the first volcanic eruption in the continental United States since 1917. It offered volcanologists a rare opportunity to study first-hand the behavior of a volcano in active eruption.

Before the Eruption

Mount St. Helens is a rather young volcano in the Cascade Range of mountains that stretches 100 miles (160 km) down the Pacific Coast, from British Columbia in Canada, through Washington and Oregon, and into northern California. There are about fifteen volcanoes in the Cascade Range. Six of them, Mounts Baker, Rainier, St. Helens, Shasta, and Lassen, are still active.

These six volcanoes have been under study by volcanologists for some years. From drilled-out samples of rock taken from the slopes of Mount St. Helens, scientists learned that the mountain was born in a powerful eruption that took place about 40,000 years ago. Both tephra and lava eruptions since then have given it its typical composite shape. The eruptions occurred about every fifty to one hundred and fifty years. And old records and accounts show that the last period of activity was between 1831 and 1857, when there were fourteen separate eruptions.

Since 1857 the volcano has been very quiet. Volcanologists believed that the mountain would erupt again. But they expected that at most it would be a mild explosion. No one expected anything large or destructive. Never in its 40,000-year history of on-again, off-again volcanic activity had the peak erupted violently.

The Approaching Eruption

Early in 1980, the glacier-covered, magnificently forested Mount St. Helens began to shake with localized earthquakes. The volcanologists detected these earth tremors on a number of portable seismometers that they had planted around the mountain. The delicate instruments picked up vibrations showing that rocks beneath the volcano were shifting and cracking, probably because of a rising flow of magma.

Earthquakes, or seismic activity, always precede the eruption of a volcano. The eruption usually occurs after a number of quakes have been detected with their centers closer and closer to the surface. But not all earthquakes are followed by volcanic eruptions. An increase in seismic activity in 1978 under Mount Shasta, for example, simply ended after a while without any eruption.

Scientists also noted that the northern slope of Mount St. Helens was beginning to bulge or swell in the mid-1970s. They

Volcanologists used portable seismometers on the slopes of Mount St. Helens to detect localized earthquakes.

knew that as magma forces its way up towards the surface just before eruption, it often pushes out the sides of the volcano. This leads the slope to tilt and the level of the land to rise.

A volcano bulge is something like what happens to the crust while you are baking an apple pie. As the pie bakes, the crust protrudes in places. Then, if the inner pressure grows too strong, the crust breaks and the juices inside come pouring out.

On the basis of their findings of seismic activity and bulges on the slopes of Mount St. Helens, the volcanologists in 1976 issued a report stating: "In the future Mount St. Helens will probably erupt violently. . . ." While they could not be specific, they did say it would most likely occur before the year 2000.

From August 1979 until April 1980 the volcanologists' instruments showed that parts of the mountain rose an amazing 320 feet (98 m). Although an eruption appeared likely, most expected to see even more change in level before the actual explosion.

The Eruption

It was exactly 8:32 A.M. on the morning of May 18, 1980, when a powerful earthquake rocked the land around Mount St. Helens. And it was precisely seven minutes later that the mountain exploded in a major volcanic eruption. The blast was Vulcanian in intensity.

In an instant, the top 1,300 feet (390 m) of the 9,677-foot (2,900-m) mountain disappeared. A pillar of hot ash and glowing gas rose about 12 miles (19 km) over the churning volcano. The noise of the explosion could be heard for hundreds of miles.

Just before the eruption, David Johnson, a thirty-year-old scientist with the U.S. Geological Survey, was on duty at a watch station on the north slope of the volcano. He was busy making observations on the bulge when the mountain let loose its full fury. Seeing no chance to escape, Johnson radioed headquarters at Vancouver with the terse message: "Vancouver, Vancouver. This is it!" Then his radio went dead.

Volcanologists say that the mountain exploded from the buildup of gas and magma that had caused the bulge on the northern slope. The explosion was triggered by the earthquake that came just before it.

The tremor caused a landslide that, as one scientist said, popped the cork of rock holding in the magma. The violence was increased by the chemistry of the mountain's rock, which was silica-rich and therefore thick and heavy. Thus the dissolved gases could not easily escape. When the surface was finally ruptured, the pent-up forces were released with fantastic energy.

A group of six friends were camping near the base of Mount St. Helens on the day it erupted. As they were cooking breakfast, they suddenly felt a blast of searing heat. Within seconds a thick, heavy rain of hot ash threatened to bury them where they stood. The bright day grew as dark as a starless night. Trees crashed to the ground around them. As they tried to dig their way out of the fallen ash, they were burned and seared by its intense heat.

The dust in the air turned to mud in their mouths, and the awful-smelling gas from the volcano made them gag. The larger

The mountain erupted with the force of a 50-megaton hydrogen bomb on the morning of May 18.

—58

hunks of ash struck them hard, raising ugly welts and painful bruises on their bodies.

After some hours, the clouds of volcanic dust drifted away, and the darkness lifted. Two of the six were dead. Another was badly burned; charred skin hung in strips from his chest and back. The sixth camper was pinned under a fallen tree.

Two of the survivors set out in search of help. They walked for ten hours over 15 miles (24 km) of what one called a "white-hot desert" of ash. Finally they were spotted by a helicopter that rescued them and the two others who were still at the campsite.

The volcano continued to erupt without stop for four days. Then the force of the eruptions began to weaken, although the volcano still shot out tall jets of steam and occasional puffs of ash and dust. The job of measuring the damage began. Over the next few weeks, search parties combed the wilderness. They found the bodies of thirty-two people, who were killed either by the first blast, by the fall of ash, or by a plunging mud flow. Another thirty people are still missing and are assumed to be dead.

About 1,000 people were evacuated from the area. Some 370,000 were put out of work as a result of the eruption. And millions more in the entire northwestern corner of the United States suffered in one way or another.

Many people, for example, were stranded in their cars or houses for days. Some individuals saw their homes badly damaged or destroyed; others suffered ruin of farmland or loss of income because their place of business was closed. Officials estimate the total cost of this one incident to be in excess of $2.7 billion!

Much of the destruction right around Mount St. Helens was due to the power and heat of the blast itself and by the mud flows that barreled down the slopes. About 150 square miles (390 sq km) of fir tree forests were completely flattened. A pilot who flew over the area of felled trees said it looked to him "as if some giant had combed his hair." Lakes and streams near the summit were choked with volcanic dust and became big, ugly mudholes.

Damage and destruction in places hundreds or thousands of miles away was largely caused by massive quantities of dust delivered by the winds. In the area of Moscow, Idaho, for instance, 300 miles (480 km) from Mount St. Helens, about 8 tons (7.2 m.t.) of volcanic ash fell on every acre of land.

The gritty dust got into everything. People coughed and sneezed. They complained of dry, itchy noses, sore throats, and painful, red eyes. One man said the dust made him feel as though someone had taken his eyeballs and rolled them around in a sandbox. Many fish in rivers were killed, either by the raised temperature of the water or because their gills were clogged with ash. A large part of the insect population was destroyed, too, eventually causing the birds that lived on the insects to die in great numbers also.

After the Eruption

The week following the eruption was relatively quiet, though gases and clouds of ash still escaped from time to time. Then, on May 25, another big eruption hit, though not as violent as the first one. A number of other eruptions followed in the summer and fall. Based on what they know about volcanoes, scientists believe that these occasional eruptions may continue until nearly the end of the century.

Since the first eruptions in the spring of 1980, Mount St.

One airplane pilot said it looked to him "as if some giant had combed his hair."

Helens has virtually been swarming with volcanologists. As one put it, "Volcanoes are windows through which the scientist looks into the bowels of the earth."

Some are analyzing the gases that are coming up through cracks and openings in the sides of the volcano. Past volcano research shows that the amount of sulfur dioxide (SO_2) in the gas increases before an eruption. Although there was no increase in the percentage of sulfur dioxide between the beginning of activity and the big eruption on May 18, the SO_2 level did rise just before two of the eruptions that followed. Indeed, when the percentage of SO_2 doubled in September, scientists expected another eruption, but nothing happened. "We don't have anything that is 100 percent accurate," explained one volcanologist, somewhat philosophically.

Scientists tracking the seismic activity around the volcano noticed that the continuing earthquakes seemed to move down about 12 miles (19 km) beneath the surface right after the eruption. This led them to believe, correctly, that the danger of an eruption had lessened for a while.

Also detected was an increase in the earth's trembling on August 7. Officials ordered everyone to leave the so-called Red Zone, an area between 10 and 15 miles (16 and 24 km) from the peak of Mount St. Helens. Late that afternoon there was indeed an eruption, but because of the timely warning no one was injured.

The eruption of Mount St. Helens was a major blow for almost everyone in the state of Washington. But the human spirit has a way of finding humor even in the face of disaster. Take, for instance, the drivers around Mount St. Helens who covered part of their license plates so that they read "ASHINGTON," the baseball team that canceled its game because they were "ashed out," and the newspaper that referred to the fourth day of the eruption as "Ash Wednesday." But perhaps the best comment was seen on a sign in a bank window, many of whose customers wore handkerchiefs over their mouths and noses. The sign read, "For security reasons, please remove masks before entering the bank!"

Mount St. Helens in 1980 was the last in a long series of major eruptions that goes back to a time when the earth was very young. Just as there have been exploding volcanoes in the past, so there will be many volcanic eruptions yet to come. But as volcanologists study Mount St. Helens and the volcanoes of the past, they are coming to better understand the hows and whys of volcanoes, and someday they may find ways to curb the loss of life and destruction of property caused by these violent displays of nature.

Index